OBSCENITY FOR THE ADVANCEMENT OF POETRY

OBSCENITY FOR THE ADVANCEMENT OF POETRY

kathryn l. pringle

OMNIDAWN PUBLISHING
OAKLAND, CALIFORNIA
2017

Cover art by Violette Quintana. *Untitled.*

Cover typeface: Cronos Pro & Adobe Caslon Pro
Interior typeface: Minion Pro

Cover & interior design by Cassandra Smith

Offset printed in the United States
by Edwards Brothers Malloy, Ann Arbor, Michigan
On 55# Enviro Natural 100% Recycled 100% PCW
Acid Free Archival Quality FSC Certified Paper

Library of Congress Cataloging-in-Publication Data

Names: Pringle, Kathryn L., author.
Title: Obscenity for the advancement of poetry / Kathryn L. Pringle.
Description: Oakland, California. : Omnidawn Publishing, 2017.
Identifiers: LCCN 2017020881 | ISBN 9781632430427 (pbk. : alk. paper)
Classification: LCC PS3616.R548 A6 2017 | DDC 811/.6--dc23
LC record available at https://lccn.loc.gov/2017020881

Published by Omnidawn Publishing, Oakland, California
www.omnidawn.com   (510) 237-5472   (800) 792-4957
10 9 8 7 6 5 4 3 2 1
ISBN: 978-1-63243-042-7

acknowledgments:

my eternal respect and gratefulness to and for Rusty Morrison for her dedication, insight, and uncanny ability to keep this poet's fire lit and hold the vision for this manuscript even when i could not. these poems could not have been written without syd staiti, erin wilson, gillian conoley, terry ehret, stacy doris, suzanne stein, rebecca stoddard, elise ficarra, andrea rexillius, danielle pafaunda, christine cody, the old Lucipo gang, michael nicoloff, and barbara jane reyes. extra special thanks and love to amanda...because everything.

deep gratitude to the editors of the following journals and presses for publishing previous versions and parts of this manuscript: *Coldfront*, *Denver Quarterly*, Duration Press, *Epiphany*, *Everyday Genius*, *La Petite Zine*, *Lavender*, *Mrs. Maybe*, *Manor House*, *Phoebe*, *Saginaw*, & *Sidebrow*.

for Geneva Chao

table of contents

across dialectics scholars blow red ammunitions of truth. it's

rust. clearer in sediment from rain (no one breaks sail when

endurance is water) hail limitations part the wind the way

blackbirds cannot anchors would not end reason if shifting

never moves everything to how one thing is happens perhaps

it is of dust not of waves the streams that so far up the stars

weren't stars when then into a little box, another comes

flaming in one truth of all there   that there. there. but then

the one arrives who struggles longer poor all who cannot know

how first another ends rusting like truth its dust   blows

across anchors shifting streams of how one thing is into a box

of truth the scholars dust the reason of ammunitions, hail

dialectics in rain that stream the way blackbirds   in wind

the endurance of stars that weren't   in any way   in any

season there is rain   there is ammunition   there is rust

that moves all things across sediment   poor scholars of

shifting reason: waves little truth happens dialectics.

obscenity for the advancement of poetry 1

cerebral trash

a list:: a preselected violence:: a table of contents

one cigarette
one horoscope
one raid

one dubiously obtained mathematical field

conversely – at the top of the ladder one could see the future –

//barely-lifted fog//

MISTAKE'S a question of occasion
                              the window a television

receding perpetually

the undertaken

merging in syntax to preserve

distinction: a river's mouth

that urge to conduct, simulate
stimulation of the pistol
[itchy trigger] fingered
a conjured cellular connection

:i don't care about the walls anymore:

unsure. under searching. about the glue
an appraisal, holding us not so far off

thank the war

:i'm trying to give up utterance:

this is how we cope with modernity // it forgives us of bombs

The White Room

The walls of the room are white and the furniture in the room is white, too. The sound of the room is white and the woman in the room is white, too. The boxing of the television is white but the screen of the television is black-and-white static—no station found static with the sound of buzzing white. The woman lies on the bed, dressed in white, torso propped up by pillows. Staring. Presumably at the screen.

Her face is blank. Expressionless. Her eyes are vacant. If she is capable of thought, she is probably deep in thought, and perhaps somewhere else completely. A white door with a white-framed opened slot is to her left. It is closed. The door. The white-framed opened slot has a tray with plates of food on it. Steam can be seen in the light rising from the food, but the woman will not see it. She shows no interest in the food or the room or the television.

The light in the room does not come from the sun.

Three rows of fluorescent recessed troffers provide light for the room. It is cold light. The woman does not appear to feel things like heat and cold.

The white noise continues to penetrate the room. The tray of food continues to go unnoticed. The woman in white continues being inside herself. She has swallowed herself. The white noise her hypnotist.

Before her is an immense winding staircase. Its polished wooden bannisters seem to go into the upper atmosphere, beyond the attic of the old building whose doors she has entered into.

It is dark inside.

Dust covers everything but the polished bannisters. She does not find this odd. Each step is carpeted. It is a grand staircase and she knew if she mounted it, if she had the strength, it would lead her to somewhere very special. Somewhere necessary.

She stands at the foot of the staircase and looks around. She feels a cold gust of wind, but there are not any windows in sight.

The room she is in is dark.

The only light seems to come from her own body—she is glowing. A faint light can be seen somewhere toward the top of the staircase, or what she assumes to be the top.

She hesitates.

The feeling she has is not fear but she wants to use that word. It is not sadness, but she could use that word, too. Desperation. Trepidation. Ecstasy. Each suitable and inaccurate. Useless, intentionless words. She has no audience. None that she is aware of. Why bother with the word?

The woman, the glowing pale woman in white, remains still at the bottom of the staircase for several moments. Around her: motes of dust, lit by her own skin—floating any which way. Filaments of her and the room dance in the glow just beyond her skin.

She is not in a room at all. The construct of "room" is something her mind automatically applied to what she could not recognize in her surroundings. Recognize or acknowledge? There is no room only space. The staircase is real. The glow is not. The filaments, the motes—real. The polished wood—not. The surface is not polished. It is filthy rough. Were she to reach out and allow herself to feel—she would feel the scraping of splintered wood. She would feel the splinters under skin, hear the crunching of peeled and chipped paint underfoot, and smell

the mold and mildew in the air. But she does not.

obscenity for the advancement of poetry 2

claustrophobic intoxication / fucking police

[I cannot write myself
out of this place.   no
matter   how hard I
try. not to   think of
environment   as con
tainment. I am   not
able to write   myself
out of this   city. I am
not of transplant-trans
ient.]

the sun laked itself upon waking
the plaza poisoned
how to speak freely when "free"

civil engineering part I

when you says i

i means me

and the place that holds

that is being held

with

me, that is

being

held with

not by

systemic identity:

       automated self

:a person context

the event of

           invention:

a lyric of

spiraled light and gaunt veins

dragging behind

the cartography wrested
in what was
is what is. we was
—i loves value
the envy in it
the deep cut of it

      an expense, it is,
when the other calls you
     sweet

the cruel cringe of fact
nestles into your side
a sightless Ciacco rising

the circle was made before you were here
yet you argue its existence—

giving voice to the creature of it

position

in place

it fits

a to-be
situated

       the becoming of the event that takes me
is the unraveling of the she that was

when young, i do this:
take what is ready. accept what is never

enough. all in the name of
perpetuity—
       even what i share with you

a dampness of lungs

a small percentage of the population would incise
gills if
needed

moan on yr back
curl up

      loathing integrity
yr pillows
      yr sheets

is need

to be no
self
to be
imagined
to awaken out
of joy
a cold twin
mattress

the barren body, held stiff

breaks light
against the empty shelves

but the thing is
the contract is
finite. but we signed to
disbelieving, parasympathetic, and all
hung out
the cardiac flags
of the firmly entrenched
we knows they never waver

this is the constitutional remix
this is reality by consensus
that we is within. us's inevitable lurch–
the rector of us's equanimity
questions are acceptable now
accepted, expected

and
this

        inevitable

                ubiquitous

     lurch

the physiological need

for conflict
inflates at the ready
as does the need for control
an action we
must be able to see
to exit
the work of
the STATE
a camouflage

deliberate patterned action

we the plundered
we the pained
we of the generically prescribed
too burdened to afford the luxury
of our legally gerrymandered communities
too burdened with the business that is
holding THEMS up

we, the electorate imagination
a house of mirrors

IT REFLECTS YOU
        it "yous" it

our WE speech speaks slant

an officially sanctioned
REALITY

how we copes

postmodernity—it is of
corporations chemicals
and implanted NEED

and o, AFTER ALL THAT HONEY
can we not avow it
truly?

fate can do us
its designers
specialize in resource acumen
monetary shrapnel
we is a consumer
we is civility enforcer
a voter and a letter

with direct windows
out the sides of

THOSE
SUPERIOR MOUTHS

the prearranged jaws

us's constructs pulse red
            and again
us's bodies spin
to fit dictation

only the broken remain

holding vigilante
the broken glass
the broken bodies
the broken illusions
of our pleas
our signs

our never-ending rally
against ourselves
lining the streets

til the negotiation branded avenues
US's ground lengthened

the dark body ethos
must learn the boundary
ludic alms
a serenade of arms
       scapes enter over
       tongue erring
       tongue rotten
            a bitter vocal

at the waking scapes for feel
tongues like dancers
                 frame and punkture

i or i

stanching a stricken vein

the trick fallen

and all i
is i

ostensibly
virtually

a steady sound

so we are done
go ahead and enter the passage
go so that phrases and references

                           can enter you

a public composition
a text on thought
the appellate
a small, extraordinary
responder
roulette is one line
                interrupted by apologies

what is known of lungs:

surfactant is essential

what it means to break the attractive forces of water molecules
to water molecules – water will always choose water over air –

EXPANSION

does space form
or does
a new place
present
itself

where
        now
                broken
        bond?

there is an alternative
to rupture
but since we
are attached to breath
let it go unsaid

one tenable gasp

for us to hold
tension's surface : a void pulled taut

i keep choosing inaction
watching it all cede
my skin a shoreline forever giving way

each moment a slipping

there will be so much less of my present self soon

not a drowning
an erosion

some would rather burn

as if we get to choose

but some would rather burn
others fall

i keep letting things go

perhaps foolishly

or needlessly

i was taught it poor manners to take
no matter how desirable
something from someone

anything from someone
but mostly something

this particular tendency has resulted in my own diminishing

at one point in this story, i was magnanimous
you will have to take my word for it

beyond reproach
incredibly pure

i was radiant

but, we gathered not

a struggle

if there is no space

as established prior, there is no place

then either one vanishes

or moves elsewhere

which amounts to the same thing from the other's perspective

although, vanishing has its more painful consequences:

neverness, being the most formidable

how to get someone to speak what's true

i just wants

resilience – vulnerability = cold

post
ictal
menace

maybe it is permanent

I KNOW IT IS BROKEN JUST IGNORE IT.

      practicing silence

      or refusal

yes, no.

yes.

sitting in emptiness is not the same as sitting in void

there is no abyss, except for maybe the internal

obscenity for the advancement of poetry 3

of the 4-legged:

he had over 150 engorged ticks covering his dog body by the time they found him. ticks with half an inch of pus covering their black bodies. they were sucking him to death. the dog was a boy named Sheila. he could no longer move without wanting to die. snout covered with pus-covered ticks. long german shepherd snout. they were sucking the life out of him. he lived in the basement. his mother lived on the 3rd floor. it was queens. or flushing. she didn't notice anything was wrong. he was 30% underweight. he was living in a basement that in california would be called a crawl space. he had fleas. he was going to die. the dog named Sheila. they found him. they had to remove every tick with tweezers. they put them on butcher paper and they butchered the ticks of Sheila. the blood of Sheila popped out of their asses.

Sheila moved to the village after that.

The White Room

The woman sought an explanation for her location. She fashioned her surroundings into a room. But she had no clue as to how she traveled to the place that she was in. She had no memory of where she was before that moment. Who she was before that moment. She was able to accept the room, staircase, and her own body draped in white and glowing light, but unable to accept that nothing but the future or the present was before her. Perhaps her reason for not bounding up the stairs toward the other light was reticence. She wanted to know who she was. What she would be ascending the staircase from. Some part of her wanted to know truths.

The woman placed her right foot on the first step. The step felt solid and more real than her own flesh. She looked behind herself. All she could see was darkness. She listened for a sound that was not there. A sound that—for a reason she did not recall— she missed, not because it was especially lovely but because she had always known it to be there. Instead she heard nothing. It made her feel colder, somehow. Forlorn.

The thought occurs to her, and she cannot dismiss it, that *there* could be anywhere now that *here* was anywhere. She knew she was in a new place. Could that place be so entirely new that she was without referents—all referents being applicable only in her former, forgotten-but-for-sound, place?

She looked at her naked foot on the step.

She lifted her foot and placed it in one violent motion.

She felt the pressure of it.

It made no sound.

civil engineering part II

nothing is so quiet as when a writer sits in emptiness

in and with

another writing in another room of the same house sitting in the
same emptiness

is it the same?

perhaps

we made it together

the beginning of things was perfect
we devolved
from there

it will take one revolution to get back to that

yet unshared emptiness

should it be

shared

but no
that would make a place
out of the emptiness
a place in the space of it

and we are reluctant writers
of the empty

not the impetus
not the energy
made for revolution

will we
will we

not

one word

has come of the empty

not-words, purposeful not-words

the folding amino acids of our sentence

during this time, i have learned the ceiling is discolored

birds are raucous morning creatures

the neighbors like to yell FUCK more than they actually fuck

somewhere nearby there is a screeching monkey

out the window is a gray Oakland

the city of my displacement

the daily decentering of me in such geography

it has caused age to surface on my skin

and hair

it is beautiful

inescapable

or maybe i have resigned myself

given notice to who i was

THIS IS NOT WHO YOU WILL BE

it reads

once i was very proud

and then the emptiness settled into me

now i know where others turn to whiskey

i turn empty

worse than betrayal is the righteousness of the betrayed

this is what i think of myself: you are too righteous

forgiveness, i know, it wins me back

if i forgive, i can foster my own joy again

but what a bitter cold streak in the center of me

such a deep desire to punish

one thing to know it
another to know why

what do you know
of my lungs

what of my breathing
my expansiveness
or pulmonary life

in the pockets of yr lungs
the tiniest fragments
penetrating
careful not to puncture

a stick in the ribs

that's what it feels like

a stick in the ribs

to care about humans

the you that you are left with as it fades

not the you as you are when the connection arrives

the you that feels the vacuum of space inside yr body

the charge—which burned so large—burnt itself out

hollowed you

and now what took little effort
is a memory of ease almost unbearable to remember now

yr lungs are normal

what do you know of   my lungs?
"they are normal"

space contained

a subliminal parsing of direct address

the significance of "pink streaks" in the sky

over a body of water

quantify feeling

that time 1+1+1+1 equaled 1

too many ones untrained
in the art of being two

i know i have to lose
you again but i can't

outside my skin

so little matters

the spoken scapes enter over the tongue
[a barked vocal]
tongue rising [branded] [the medium of vocal]
all of it pipes, chords, mucous [memory]

at the place of voice, their village, at that ending
and misperception of what some striker said
the friendly puncture hovers

the lungs lift

    for longing

        voicing

          i

        and

         o

after rolling over and squaring back
on all four, a syllabic juggernaut

straining
aching for repetition
the vedic trachea

      i and
      then *o*

the infinite loop that is Lake Merritt
the solace it offers the heartbroken,
the downtrodden
the night herons
the illness of intent
momentarily departed

only to return

the debt of
utterance

bears
down

once again
    in speaking
    in breath

a tree folds over the falling
ignorance a reckoning of vision

a sign
the stilling veins

an open someone
forgets environment
forgets or becomes

a forensic seer

the future as it was seen
then
remembering so

owns vocalization
a tale sprung and bated
a grandiose schemata
tilling each chord
mining each synapse

what we forgets is blood carries everything through us
binding us to ourselves, other selves, nonselves

the practice of flowing

half tremolos, darling,

value yourself over Helen.
dance made still

delighted by spoken sight
annulled through language
through fucks and eeks
come to same

vocals linger between *vak* and *strek*
over them *as.*

how do you befolk the people?

all they wanted to do was get fucked

the dream said that one would die
the other inherit money
but the two weren't linked
the two events, supposedly
the two people yes, but not the events

two people are linked but the events occurring
around them are not. they are 'unrelated'

the two people are related but the two events accruing
around the two people are not

the events are apparently related but the two people around
which the accruing events are not

people like to sing when they are alone
they like to shower and sing but not so loud
everyone dances when nobody is looking
everyone sings and dances
every body has body inside their bodies
every body moves within its own interstitial fluids
every body inside of bodies dances and sings when no body is
looking
the blind body

to be observed by another is to be defined
we takes care to be observant
when you fuck a woman you are not necessarily a man
when you fuck a woman you are not necessarily a human
when you fuck a woman you are not necessarily a you
when fucking women
effort goes a long way

do not forget yrself when fucking women
do not forget to fuck yrself when fucking women
do not forget to fuck while fucking yrself
do not forget to do it right
do not forget to
reach around

the thing is
the contract is binding
only if we is bound

the lifting yielding

the slide follows down through the course

of veins and tendons and ligaments

tissues

connecting

self to self

but not one to another

that being reserved for

water and air

The White Sprawl

If they think of me at all it is simply as an address.

As representative of this property which is esteemed worthless.

Nothing to see here, nothing to see here say police.

I reach for a fresh bottle. It is a still afternoon. The sun is shining and insects are buzzing but most humans have been removed from my immediate environment.

I like days like this. They make for a rare peace.

I sit in my chair staring out my open window.

Some humans are moving somewhere. I can hear their motors in the distance—atmospheric perspective—their sounds as near as the blued mountains are far. It doesn't bother me to hear them far off. It is reassuring to know they are there, and away. I just want to sit here and not move a while. I feel so finished with motion.

Stillness fills me. It breathes me. To have space and to hold it so carefully as to cultivate stillness is an art. Hard to create with humans.

I close my eyes. The outside of me sounds as if it is inside of me.

My body began to fail when the houses began to deconstruct. Immediate weakening. I am sitting in one of the few houses that have remained still. The sky isn't any different than it was before all the changes. Before my body began to fail. But the water is quite different. It has a tacky composition. You can pull it like cooling wax.

In the meadow that is now but used to be a department store I found a pipe leaking water that still looks like water. This is what I drink when I'm not drinking bourbon. Bourbon is medicinal; everyone knows this.

The stillness is lovely. It leaves room for the pain of my body. I think maybe I can't be dead yet because I can still feel pain. Referred pain: A toast to the invisible humans of sound in the distance… Pain is the most exquisite part of this silence.

The birds. They do nothing but hover.

Nothing but hover.

obscenity for the advancement of poetry 4

SILVER DOLLARS

:rumour: one: trial

Two pink streaks last Saturday
First Response™ strips
[secret revealed]
One bottle
      A Waste
[no, I]
      will pay this.

six pabst blue ribbons and one bottle of jim beam

:2:

APHASIA

:lie # 3: gutter

deliberate

absence

she says –

she says –

HISTORICALLY AMBIVALENT

AMBIVALENCE/HISTORY

:shape #4: good judgment is clearly an ability or acquaintance

the man pushed the woman against the wall
that the woman chose to be pushed against
the man who was not gay pushed the woman
who was drunk against the man that she
chose to rub up against two weeks before

the woman's wife came home from Bloomingdales.
_ d Mann drücken d Frau gegen d Wand daß d Frau wählen zu
sein drücken gegen d Mann sein nicht homosexuell drücken d
Frau sein trinken gegen d Mann daß sie wählen zu reiben oben
gegen zwei Wochevor d Frau Frau kommen

Haus von Bloomingdales. _
_ D man press D woman against D wall that D woman select to be
press
against D man its not homosexual press D woman its drink
against D man that it select to rub above against two week before
D Mrs. woman come house of Bloomingdales. _

:whopper #5: "my bikini waxer. she's Brazilian."

I am carrying the child cat where my uterus is small.

Crying at hallmark cards.

Fearing encroachment.

:burden #6: one rough return

'yr breasts look huge.'

'pms'

'not due so soon.'

'eating too much'

'   '

'   '

:perjure[†]: how to serve yr neighbor

indulge in abuse and backchat
while sipping her fine teas–fasting

        bloodletting
          back home

we are polite: caviar and corned beef
             aside.

:ate:LIBERTY: **JUST.**

"we have already forbidden madness
and the representation of madness."

               –Plato, *The Republic*

:nine: license: dramatic recitation

in pink, the decent man of opposite character occupies a tolerant
position whilst wagering

bulls bellowing and roaring sexuality upon before behaving stead-

iness and determination owing to illness [love] indulgence [drink]
indifference [appetite]

but we argued. so i threw him into the fondue and spread him over
a nice crisp.

:fiction: cock and bull: #10: i get sick, but i'm happier.

when i was 12 he was 18 and had two bullet holes in his chest he
waited for my parents to leave me and climbed the lemon tree
through my street facing bedroom window ~~i wouldn't saying
anything nor thoughting this~~ he said he would open his mouth
and buttermilk would flow from those bullet holes but i just closed
my eyes and pretended he was the Virgin Mary.

civil engineering part III

Calistoga
for staiti

the snap
center squared, carries the suggestion
of fatigue
wakes to eyelids
                              upper/lower
puffed beyond their usual borders
eyes
the antidote to so much affront
but one can only bluff one's
self for so long
before the girder snaps

it wasn't built for this kind

in photographs everyone always seems
to be on the verge of something

not a precipice: a verge

it won't make sense in ten years

it will still carry the embarrassment of its time

but in twenty

it will be what keeps us together

that moment
in the sun
when the grapes did not grow
but we had wine
          and mud
anyway

QUERELLE
after Schroeter

the man might be naked
his torso is bending
he is slim and hairy

his hair isn't bothering me, I'm just noticing
his torso is covered with dark hair

he is muscular

he has the posture of a dancer

he is making moves like he knows how to dance

he is smiling

he has that moustache

that gay moustache

from the 1970s

the women are on stage and the sailors are in love

with each other. one woman is dancing and another woman is
holding a sword

in a crouched position. both women are on stage.

do they see each other? the sailors are in love.

they are kissing each other gazing

into the eyes of each other with love. one sailor is the dancer

with the moustache and the hairy torso. the other sailor is less
hairy.

but I'm not sure

they are in sailor uniforms, hat and all, and each other's arms

in the first chairs

in what are representative of the first of many chairs in the first of
many rows

before the stage

you can see the woman dancer

she is dancing in the space between their mouths

she is dancing in the space behind their mouths, too

this is a very long scene.

the sailors come together and then, at arm's length, they part to
gaze

they are so happy

it is hard to know if the dancing woman has feelings about love

[prayer]

we sit in a circle (on folding chairs
            at the other end the branches of trees)

  white men scream and then a sound   I hadn't heard
the trees smoking   the glass fracture   I could discern
pipes when humans
      running down stairs
             running pulse

not consumed   meant the women could sing

static other and stillness   not the oldest but the most
skillful minutes
     equaled one
         twenty
   a future
       (I   would roll phonetic forms from tongue call
   the "authorities")
       and this is three thirty am,

would those in understanding   respond

[prayer]

light steps in the room [twenty]
        a child running between my parents
who sometimes
                then white noise
disconnected the line

sat side by side forgiven, for being
cell and human
    shattered
    child forgiven for being child

later men would dance
                white
with lemons from the yard   handkerchiefs in a circle
    soft and rotting

/layers/ to describe a thing by its shadow

that big giant head is dodgy, the dolls desperate for rolling
down clamor notes drumming Columbus past tracks yellow
costumed skid marks men honking horns   dust
thrown sheepish firecrackers at Washington   an illusionist
holds still empty the shadow passenger of Transamerica red
flags disillusion flashlights chanting
[the motorcycle cops staring down words
[white helmets / black strapped words
        loudspeakers imagining field and phonic symbols
hoodwink bleeding light vapor bulb   sponsored newscast
magician (for hire)
desperate report of truthfulness w / parade outline

head bandage replete with hole

[loose change on cigarette scarred park bench]

she is tagged at the wrist
a suitcase on a passenger plane
left hand drawn up
in the universal sign of
I have a headache

she balances without effort

on the evidence available

the captain of the ship upon which the body was found termed the
incident 'unlucky.' he went on to state that several of his men were
frolicking with abandon throughout the night and could not be
roused for questioning at this time.

it appears that the woman's body is that of a civilian, between the
ages of 20 and 25.

obscenity for the advancement of poetry 5

those motherfuckers only take indecent photographs
of ice blinks.

there's a stitch in my rib it is mobile it has been there for a week it
is hard not to lie down with a stitch / secure all the rooms / sleep
in front of the closet and ignore wind

erasure is synaptic gesture / when i die i hope it will not be soon
and not from cancer / someone tried to kill her / he bought guns
and video

taped himself making a bomb mailer for her / my wash basin is
covered with toothpaste which is unfortunate because otherwise it
is such a lovely, green color / was it the right's
decision? enraging white house canines / pasture / if i listened
maybe / but we are still manipulating you and squaring off /

o maybe they will take a cross-section of my lung freeze half then
sputter off OFF: i am a soldier in my own military / in my house
the war is always on/ more details/ more loosen up ARMY / you
author my law school is painful and grotesque so returned to the
high desert where / ALLEGEDLY // what would egedly mean /
that city was poison and i've done what i can do / escape you it
must be legitimized // it is taking so long / a file that is corrupted /
our name LEXICON/

A White Room's White Noise

We are here to share an investment opportunity with you... the presentation began. Outside light was blocked by the conference room windows' vertical blinds. The blinds, which were white, suggested that the windows ran along the entire wall opposite the only door through which participants and presenters (the presenters were assumed to be present though no introductions had been made and the filtered light of the projector could be seen coming from a hole in the wall across from the large white screen the presentation was projected upon) could access the room. Each slat of the vertical blinds was haloed by a golden yellow light giving the impression of a truly beautiful morning happening outside the conference room walls.

Welcome to the offices of Standard Life Investments by F.F. Hoser & Company. We here at SLI are seriously interested in your life. Your life means something to us.

Appearing behind the words flashing on the screen were images the company believed appropriately portrayed life. The first image was of a newborn baby with wisps of black hair wrapped in a Soft As Can Be™ blue blanket. The blanket's tag was conveniently placed in the exact center of the image's frame. It read, in small font that one would normally not read thinking the words were simply telling the owner how to launder the blanket so as not to ruin its Soft As Can Be-ness:

THIS IS ONLY THE BEGINNING.

We all want your little bundle of joy to have every opportunity in life. Here at SLI by F.F. Hoser & Company, we strive to give you the biggest and best returns for your investment, so your little one will never have to worry.

This is the beginning of the rest of her life.

The baby with dark wispy hair and the Soft As Can Be Blanket has turned its head a little, opened its eyes, and giggled.

The people in the conference room did not allow any outward sign of an emotional response to register upon their faces. They held their heads straight, eyes focused upon the images and words projected on the screen in front of them, despite the fact that they were all sitting around a conference room table in largely uncomfortable positions. It was almost as if each person in the room could not bring themselves to acknowledge the fact that they had yet to purchase life insurance for themselves or their families. As if they felt such deep shame about having been so lax in the area of family-crisis management and preparation that they knew, had they made eye contact with another person in that room and in that same emotional state, it would be robbing them of what little dignity they had left. And so, forty-three heads sat rigidly fixed atop forty-three bodies, some of which were twisted at forty-five to one-hundred-and-twenty-five-degree angles, eyes trained on the baby, the words, and the perfectly blue and soft blanket that they were about to ensure their babies would be wrapped in for the rest of their lives.

Each year, one out of every five families suddenly comes face to face with an uncertain life after losing their breadwinner. Don't let this happen to you.

Images of disaster began to appear on the screen. Car crashes, plane crashes, train crashes, heart attacks at the office, at the gym, in the bedroom, in a hotel room, explosions, fires, floods, acts of war, earthquakes.

One could sense the effort it took for each of those forty-three heads not to shift, tear, sniffle, and look away.

Out of respect, no eye contact was made. The lights to the conference room, which had been only partially off for the multimedia presentation, were turned all the way off. The only light in the room came from the projector and what was presumed to be the sun, outside, sneaking in around the vertical blinds.

The lights went up inside the conference room, stunning the red eyes of the participants. The projector slid itself back into the wall and closed itself off. Dazed, the participants were still wary about meeting the eyes of each other. They continued to keep their heads down as their eyes got used to the fluorescent lighting that had invaded the room.

It was an abrupt ending.

After several successive images of disaster, the words:

DO NOT LET HIS HAPPEN TO YOU

Flashed across the white screen and the lights came on.

A man in a business suit came into the conference room and handed each participant a pack of twenty to thirty papers, life insurance forms, without breaking the no-eye-contact rule and without saying a word. After each participant had his or her own packet, the man left through the same door he entered as a woman in a business suit entered with a box of black ink pens who gave each participant a pen in the same manner that the man had given each participant a packet.

She too left the room through the same door she had entered.

The participants, heads still down, sat unmoving for several minutes, unsure of how to proceed.

Then, one participant, who very much resembled the woman who had given each participant a black ink pen, slowly moved his hands to the packet and, very slowly, unsealed the packet. His breathing did not increase but became more audible. Somehow the sound of his breathing gave him a self-assured and reassuring air. He removed the pages from the envelope and placed them neatly on the conference table.

His movement inspired others to follow suit, and soon each participant had the documents before him or herself, head bowed in silent reading.

The language on the page was stilted and foreign to the participants who had been lulled into the presentation's simple language of warning. And yet, their inability to comprehend the words before them prevented them even more from raising their heads and making eye contact with one another. The only words they could read were instructional:

Sign here. Date. Age of Dependent. Age of spouse. Smoker/ Nonsmoker. Former Smoker? How long?

Not wanting to appear any more foolish and uneducated than they already felt like they appeared due to their lack of forward thinking up until this very moment regarding their families and life insurance and saving for the future of their children, they each kept their heads down, turning pages silently, and, when each felt the proper amount of time it took to read twenty-eight pages thoroughly and understandably passed, picked up the black ink pens and signed their names to all the appropriate blank lines. Then, one-by-one they walked out of the conference room into the sun that they had seen awaiting them behind the blinds and into the future in which they felt they were assured.

THE STILLS

for Eden Osucha

1.

                         only a small blur
            of a country maybe critical   a charge intersecting seed
and rotes
                 no b&w gas station or flags crossing
            railroads all dust and blown
                         now no river   left to tumble

                         a sequence is a decade
                         in the passing person–

                         operates the thorax nerves project

2.

two black labs against a dense wall of conifers next to interstate 85

wonder if stopping
will only make it worse

we drive / you

towards the war

America's Rome is Baltimore
see shelled-out ruins of snitches

3.

she's telling about the trees

used for lynching

used to be called HANGTOWN

east is east
but this is west

there are live oaks in the west
and a town not called HANGTOWN
now, but was, in the west

now named for a lake
a pleasant, simple life

this is we by extension

an emptiness here where once was
a culture, a citizen, a life

no restitution.

4.

it is falling down outside and blocking the drive.
in pieces at a time. gun shots sound out
we drive passing them //

soft landings

yesterday's trees sagged. i think it means you miss

today the wind is not moving faster than the car

it looks awfully thick
to be an allegory

my spectacle tells me Memphis is running
i mean it is on my mind–the fear in it

5.

to stall o but the heat

        Memphis
          thick with it

the way-fried pickles [as in over]
and graceland only hazard

we, a determination of how one can

      be so
light   about light

the bricks writ with // are pleading for life

6.

the lungs gurgle
labored
near to drown
in that room
in this one
he cannot breathe
his trachea is
collapsing
but still he will
dance for you
at the typewriter

7.

in Holbrook there is nothing but sky
not money, no water
in the pool
we sat, as four, angered by the leaving

that night i dream we are living
the pain of knowing we will die
always just behind ourselves
we sink into resentful breathing

when i wake up: it is still hot
there is still no water in the pool
and we are still angry.

8.

i wish my chest would billow. the wind is blowing.

instead i buffet.

in las vegas the neighboring table told us to go to the gardens
because they were the most amazing gardens the table had ever
seen and so we go but we think hasn't that table ever been to
even this man. it doesn't occur to us that the table has ever traveled
outside of las vegas but the table is from ohio so it must've been
from somewhere else with plants. plastic motorbikes and racecars
set amongst pink plastic flowers and some. we got lost for a little
while. gambled 7 dollars that also got lost.

went back to the hotel to be with the dogs.

9.

there is no reasoning the darkness always to my left.

10.

there is only an image and the image is light
a light that is only california light what does light
do goes so appreciated in a way that only is taken
with light that is light from a thicker air   a mossier
plain. there is only image and image is awkward
stilt-split in a hat handlebarred or barren repeat
stumble fade only image and image is vulnerable
moments fingers slid in holes not meant for
sliding in too dark to believe in site-specific

an ominous tone is beshitting the poem that began with image
that is light that is only

11.

we buy Diebenkorn prints to remind us of home.

kathryn l. pringle is the author of *Temper & Felicity are Lovers* (Lost Roads Press, 2014), winner of the Besmilir Brigham Award; *fault tree* (Omnidawn, 2011), winner of the Omindawn 1st/2nd Book award; and *RIGHT NEW BIOLOGY* (Factory School, 2009). In 2013, she was awarded a grant from the Fund for Poetry and was also a Lambda Literary Award finalist. Raised in Southern California and schooled in the Bay Area, kathryn now makes her home in Durham, North Carolina.

obscenity for the advancement of poetry
by kathryn l. pringle

Cover art by Violette Quintana. *Untitled.*

Cover typeface: Cronos Pro & Adobe Caslon Pro
Interior typefaces: Minion Pro

Cover & interior design by Cassandra Smith

Offset printed in the United States
by Edwards Brothers Malloy, Ann Arbor, Michigan
On 55# Enviro Natural 100% Recycled 100% PCW
Acid Free Archival Quality FSC Certified Paper

Publication of this book was made possible in part by gifts from:
The Clorox Company
The New Place Fund
Robin & Curt Caton

Omnidawn Publishing
Oakland, California
2017
Rusty Morrison & Ken Keegan, senior editors & co-publishers
Gillian Olivia Blythe Hamel, managing editor
Cassandra Smith, poetry editor & book designer
Sharon Zetter, poetry editor, book designer & development officer
Avren Keating, poetry editor, fiction editor & marketing assistant
Liza Flum, poetry editor
Juliana Paslay, fiction editor
Gail Aronson, fiction editor
Trisha Peck, marketing assistant
Cameron Stuart, marketing assistant
Natalia Cinco, marketing assistant
Maria Kosiyanenko, marketing assistant
Emma Thomason, administrative assistant
SD Sumner, copyeditor
Kevin Peters, *OmniVerse* Lit Scene editor
Sara Burant, *OmniVerse* reviews editor